for Advent and the Christmas Season 2020–21

SACRED SPACE

November 29, 2020 to January 10, 2021

from the website www.sacredspace.ie
Prayer from the Irish Jesuits

LOYOLA PRESS.
A JESUIT MINISTRY
Chicago

LOYOLA PRESS.
A JESUIT MINISTRY

3441 N. Ashland Avenue
Chicago, Illinois 60657
(800) 621-1008
www.loyolapress.com

Scripture quotations are from *New Revised Standard Version Bible: Catholic Edition*, copyright © 1989, 1993 National Council of the Churches of Christ in the United States of America. Used by permission. All rights reserved.

Advent retreat by **Gráinne Doherty,** used with permission.

Cover art credit: oxygen/Moment/Getty Images.

ISBN-13: 978-0-8294-5015-6

Printed in the United States of America.
20 21 22 23 24 Versa 10 9 8 7 6 5 4 3 2 1

Contents

The Presence of God

Bless all who worship you, almighty God,
from the rising of the sun to its setting;
from your goodness enrich us,
by your love inspire us,
by your Spirit guide us,
by your power protect us,
in your mercy receive us,
now and always.

How to Use This Booklet

During each week of Advent, begin by reading the "Something to think and pray about each day this week." Then go through "The Presence of God," "Freedom," and "Consciousness" steps to help you prepare yourself to hear the Word of God speaking to you. In the next step, "The Word," turn to the Scripture reading for each day of the week. Inspiration points are provided if you need them. Then return to the "Conversation" and "Conclusion" steps. Follow this process every day of Advent.

The Advent retreat at the back of this book follows a similar structure: an invitation to experience stillness, a Scripture passage and reflection points, and suggestions for prayer; you may find it useful to move back and forth between the daily reflections and the retreat.

Something to think and pray about each day this week:

The terms *spiritual* and *religious* are often used interchangeably and most often when people identify themselves as "spiritual but not religious." Joseph and Mary, as they are depicted in the Christmas story in Matthew's Gospel, appear deeply spiritual. They use inner resources to overcome difficulties; these difficulties and challenges don't have to be spelled out to those of us familiar with the account of Jesus' birth. These inner resources open them to occasions when God's promptings and grace help nudge them into a safer place, even though at times comfort might tempt them to sit still in the same spot for a while.

However, the narrative in Matthew shows how deeply they are immersed in the religion of their days. Quotes from the Old Testament show how these moments are part of something greater and of which they are an important part. The two, religion and spirituality, are one. One definition of spirituality that I cannot forget is that it is the art of making connections. In our prayers and in our ponderings we try to connect with someone or something that can help us make our paths straight and find our own Immanuel, or God who is with us (Matthew 1:23). If we remain solely spiritual (if that can be done), then we are left with nothing to connect to, and good religion helps us connect deeply through its rituals, peoples, wisdom, and traditions.

Alan Hilliard, *Dipping into Advent*
Messenger Publications, 2019

The Presence of God

Dear Jesus, I come to you today longing for your presence. I desire to love you as you love me. May nothing ever separate me from you.

Freedom

Lord, grant me the grace to be free from the excesses of this life. Let me not get caught up with the desire for wealth. Keep my heart and mind free to love and serve you.

Consciousness

Where do I sense hope, encouragement, and growth in my life? By looking back over the past few months, I may be able to see which activities and occasions have produced rich fruit. If I do notice such areas, I will determine to give them time and space in the future.

The Word

God speaks to each of us individually. I listen attentively, to hear what he is saying to me. Read the text a few times, then listen. (Please turn to the Scripture on the following pages. Inspiration points are there should you need them. When you are ready, return here to continue.)

Conversation
What is stirring in me as I pray? Am I consoled, troubled, left cold? I imagine Jesus standing or sitting at my side, and I share my feelings with him.

Conclusion
Glory be to the Father, and to the Son, and to the Holy Spirit,
As it was in the beginning, is now, and ever shall be,
World without end. Amen.

Sunday November 29
First Sunday of Advent
Mark 13:33–37

Beware, keep alert; for you do not know when the time will come. It is like a man going on a journey, when he leaves home and puts his slaves in charge, each with his work, and commands the doorkeeper to be on the watch. Therefore, keep awake—for you do not know when the master of the house will come, in the evening, or at midnight, or at cockcrow, or at dawn, or else he may find you asleep when he comes suddenly. And what I say to you I say to all: "Keep awake."

- Advent begins today. We spend this time preparing for the coming of Christ into our world. He is here already, of course, but he wants to come closer. Let me be one of his points of entry by keeping awake to open the door when he knocks.

- What has Christ put me in charge of? How am I doing? Will I be delighted to see him when he comes?

Monday November 30
St. Andrew, Apostle
Matthew 4:18–22

As he walked by the Sea of Galilee, he saw two brothers, Simon, who is called Peter, and Andrew his brother, casting a net into the lake—for they were fishermen. And he said to them, "Follow me, and I will make you fish for people." Immediately they left their nets and followed him. As he went from there, he saw two other brothers, James son of Zebedee and his brother John, in the boat with their father Zebedee, mending their nets, and he called them. Immediately they left the boat and their father, and followed him.

- Simon Peter and Andrew heard the voice of Jesus as he walked by; James and John, while at their work, heeded and responded. Jesus speaks to them not in a time of retreat but meeting them at their work. What does it mean for me to work in a way that keeps me tuned in to a message that is for my salvation?

- In their everyday tasks, the apostles saw metaphors for how they would be as disciples of Jesus. Are there ways God speaks to me in my ordinary chores? How might God address me in the language of every day?

Tuesday December 1
Luke 10:21–24

At that same hour Jesus rejoiced in the Holy Spirit and said, "I thank you, Father, Lord of heaven and earth, because you have hidden these things from the wise and the intelligent and have revealed them to infants; yes, Father, for such was your gracious will. All things have been handed over to me by my Father; and no one knows who the Son is except the Father, or who the Father is except the Son and anyone to whom the Son chooses to reveal him."

Then turning to the disciples, Jesus said to them privately, "Blessed are the eyes that see what you see!

For I tell you that many prophets and kings desired to see what you see, but did not see it, and to hear what you hear, but did not hear it."

- Jesus is rejoicing because the seventy disciples whom he sent out have returned. They are ecstatic about the great things they have done in his name. Whenever I spread the word of God, I too am sharing in the mission of Jesus, and this should give me great joy.

- Our sense of wonder is strongest when we are children and the whole world is new. As we grow older, we become world-weary. We look without seeing and listen without hearing. I ask the Holy Spirit to make me sensitive to God's self-revelation in the everyday events of my life.

Wednesday December 2
Matthew 15:29–37

After Jesus had left that place, he passed along the Sea of Galilee, and he went up the mountain, where he sat down. Great crowds came to him, bringing with them the lame, the maimed, the blind, the mute, and many others. They put them at his feet, and he cured them, so that the crowd was amazed when they saw the mute speaking, the maimed whole, the lame walking and the blind seeing. And they praised the God of Israel.

Then Jesus called his disciples to him and said, "I have compassion for the crowd, because they have been with me now for three days and have nothing to eat; and I do not want to send them away hungry, for they might faint on the way." The disciples said to him, "Where are we to get enough bread in the desert to feed so great a crowd?" Jesus asked them, "How many loaves have you?" They said, "Seven, and a few small fish." Then, ordering the crowd to sit down on the ground, he took the seven loaves and the fish; and after giving thanks he broke them and gave them to the disciples, and the disciples gave them to the crowds. And all of them ate and were filled; and they took up the broken pieces left over, seven baskets full.

- Jesus "called his disciples to him." God calls us constantly; we seek him only because he sought us. Our love is a response to his preexisting love for us. Can I go to God in the confidence that he has compassion for me, as he had for the crowd? That he will heal, nourish, and sustain me, as he did the crowd?

- Jesus did not conjure the loaves and fish out of thin air. He took what was offered to him and multiplied it greatly. We must never think we have little to give others. As St. Teresa of Ávila reminds us, "Christ has no body now but yours. No hands, no feet on earth but yours. Yours are the eyes through which he looks compassion on this world. Yours are the feet with which he walks to do good. Yours are the hands through which he blesses all the world."

Thursday December 3
Matthew 7:21, 24–27

"Not everyone who says to me, 'Lord, Lord,' will enter the kingdom of heaven, but only one who does the will of my Father in heaven."

[Jesus said to his disciples,] "Everyone then who hears these words of mine and acts on them will be like a wise man who built his house on rock. The rain fell, the floods came, and the winds blew and beat on that house, but it did not fall, because it had been founded on rock. And everyone who hears these words of mine and does not act on them will be like a foolish man who built his house on sand. The rain fell, and the floods came, and the winds blew and beat against that house, and it fell—and great was its fall!"

- St. Ignatius also taught that love is expressed more in deeds than in words. Without good deeds there is no real life at all!

- This is our life: listening to the word of God and doing it. We are building up the Church, the Body of Christ, founded on the rock of Peter.

Friday December 4
Matthew 9:27–31

As Jesus went on from there, two blind men followed him, crying loudly, "Have mercy on us, Son of David!" When he entered the house, the blind men came to him; and Jesus said to them, "Do you believe that I am able to do this?" They said to him, "Yes, Lord." Then he touched their eyes and said, "According to your faith let it be done to you." And their eyes were opened. Then Jesus sternly ordered them, "See that no one knows of this." But they went away and spread the news about him throughout that district.

- The start of this encounter is in public. There are crowds around Jesus, and the blind men are caught up in the general emotion. They shout at Jesus, using a formal title, "Son of David," as though he was a powerful messianic figure dispensing health to crowds. Jesus waits until he is in the house, where he can meet the blind men in person and question their faith.

- Lord, you do not meet me as one of a multitude but face-to-face, on my own, where you can test the truth of my words, free from the illusions of mass emotion.

Saturday December 5
Matthew 9:35–10:1, 5a, 6–8

Then Jesus went about all the cities and villages, teaching in their synagogues, and proclaiming the good news of the kingdom, and curing every disease and every sickness. When he saw the crowds, he had compassion for them, because they were harassed and helpless, like sheep without a shepherd. Then he said to his disciples, "The harvest is plentiful, but the laborers are few; therefore ask the Lord of the harvest to send out laborers into his harvest."

Then Jesus summoned his twelve disciples and gave them authority over unclean spirits, to cast them out, and to cure every disease and every sickness. These twelve Jesus sent out with the following instructions: . . . "As you go, proclaim the good news, 'The kingdom of heaven has come near.' Cure the sick, raise the dead, cleanse the lepers, cast out demons. You received without payment; give without payment."

- Jesus, in this Gospel account I see you engaging with vigilant eyes and ears to the cry of the suffering world of your day. To them you were the compassionate one, bringing balm to the wounded places of their lives.

- Lord, the cries of the poor and brokenhearted are evident in the mass migration daily beamed into my living room. Let me not forget that you summon me today to be your eyes, your ears, and your hands of compassion. May I respond with loving compassion to all who come to me.

The Second Week of Advent
December 6–12, 2020

Something to think and pray about each day this week:

She was sitting in the pew beside him. They were a young couple. From the rings on their fingers, one could presume they were married. From the time the Mass started, her leg was going like blazes. It wouldn't stay still. It seemed like all the nervous energy of her life was concentrated in her right leg, and it just kept hopping up and down. Funnily enough, the opening prayer of the Mass for the Advent liturgy urged us to "resolve to run forth." . . . she looked like she was going to run forth out of the pew any time and break the land speed record!

Her leg didn't get a rest even when she sat down . . . . her knee was hopping up and down as she picked at the threads on those fashionable jeans that have holes in them. At one stage during the Mass, she put her head on his shoulder . . . . he tried to shrug her away but she put her head back. He pecked her on the forehead. It was a gentle kiss, and for a few moments the leg stopped.

I once heard someone say that the coming of Jesus to the world was akin to the Father kissing us. An intimate expression of his love, care, and concern for us, and the promise that he can do more and we can do more together. It's a love like this that gets our legs going like blazes in the right direction.

Alan Hilliard, *Dipping into Advent*
Messenger Publications, 2019

The Presence of God

Dear Jesus, as I call on you today, I realize that often I come asking for favors. Today I'd like just to be in your presence. Draw my heart in response to your love.

Freedom

God my creator, you gave me life and the gift of freedom. Through your love I exist in this world. May I never take the gift of life for granted. May I always respect others' right to life.

Consciousness

Dear Lord, help me remember that you gave me life. Teach me to slow down, to be still and enjoy the pleasures created for me. To be aware of the beauty that surrounds me: the marvel of mountains, the calmness of lakes, the fragility of a flower petal. I need to remember that all these things come from you.

The Word

The word of God comes down to us through the Scriptures. May the Holy Spirit enlighten my mind and my heart to respond to the Gospel teachings. (Please turn to the Scripture on the following pages. Inspiration points are there, should you need them. When you are ready, return here to continue.)

Conversation
What feelings are rising in me as I pray and reflect on God's word? I imagine Jesus himself sitting or standing near me, and I open my heart to him.

Conclusion
I thank God for these moments we have spent together and for any insights I have been given concerning the text.

Sunday December 6
Second Sunday of Advent

Mark 1:1–8

The beginning of the good news of Jesus Christ, the Son of God.

As it is written in the prophet Isaiah,
"See, I am sending my messenger ahead of you,
    who will prepare your way;
the voice of one crying out in the wilderness:
    'Prepare the way of the Lord,
    make his paths straight,'"

John the baptizer appeared in the wilderness, proclaiming a baptism of repentance for the forgiveness of sins. And people from the whole Judean countryside and all the people of Jerusalem were going out to him, and were baptized by him in the river Jordan, confessing their sins. Now John was clothed with camel's hair, with a leather belt around his waist, and he ate locusts and wild honey. He proclaimed, "The one who is more powerful than I is coming after me; I am not worthy to stoop down and untie the thong of his sandals. I have baptized you with water; but he will baptize you with the Holy Spirit."

• Mark paints a picture of a man, Jesus, who spends his public life doing good but is then betrayed, abandoned, captured, and crucified. How can this be the

Good News of Jesus Christ? I ask to be shown how Jesus' love transforms the pain and brings about the salvation of our world.

• I mingle with the crowds listening to John the baptizer. I know that he too suffered a violent death. Where is the good news in that? The good news is that he plays his part in the plan of salvation and bears steady witness to the light. In the wilderness of my life, I ask that I may always witness to light and truth and love.

Monday December 7
Luke 5:17–26

One day, while he was teaching, Pharisees and teachers of the law were sitting nearby (they had come from every village of Galilee and Judea and from Jerusalem); and the power of the Lord was with him to heal. Just then some men came, carrying a paralyzed man on a bed. They were trying to bring him in and lay him before Jesus; but finding no way to bring him in because of the crowd, they went up on the roof and let him down with his bed through the tiles into the middle of the crowd in front of Jesus. When he saw their faith, he said, "Friend, your sins are forgiven you." Then the scribes and the Pharisees began to question, "Who is this who is speaking blasphemies? Who can forgive sins but God alone?" When Jesus perceived their questionings, he answered them, "Why do you raise such questions in your hearts? Which is easier, to say, 'Your sins are forgiven you,' or to say, 'Stand up and walk'? But so that you may know that the Son of Man has authority on earth to forgive sins"—he said to the one who was paralyzed—"I say to you, stand up and take your bed and go to your home." Immediately he stood up before them, took what he had been lying on, and went to his home, glorifying God. Amazement seized all of them, and they glorified God and were filled with awe, saying, "We have seen strange things today."

- What an interesting, colorful, humorous, and yet life-changing scene! The man's friends are not easily put off. They use team effort and creativity to ensure that their paralyzed friend meets Jesus. An encounter happens that heals not only his body but also frees him from the paralysis of sin.

- Lord, forgiveness is a pressing need for all. Help me to do all I can to bring people to meet you and know your healing forgiveness. But let me do it sensitively!

Tuesday December 8
The Immaculate Conception of the Blessed Virgin Mary
Luke 1:26–38

In the sixth month the angel Gabriel was sent by God to a town in Galilee called Nazareth, to a virgin engaged to a man whose name was Joseph, of the house of David.

The virgin's name was Mary. And he came to her and said, "Greetings, favored one! The Lord is with you." But she was much perplexed by his words and pondered what sort of greeting this might be. The angel said to her, "Do not be afraid, Mary, for you have found favor with God. And now, you will conceive in your womb and bear a son, and you will name him Jesus. He will be great, and will be called the Son of the Most High, and the Lord God will give to him the throne of his ancestor David. He will reign over the house of Jacob forever, and of his kingdom there will be no end." Mary said to the angel, "How can this be, since I am a virgin?" The angel said to her, "The Holy Spirit will come upon you, and the power of the Most High will overshadow you; therefore the child to be born will be holy; he will be called Son of God. And now, your relative Elizabeth in her old age has also conceived a son; and this is the sixth month for her who was said to be barren. For nothing will be impossible with God." Then Mary said, "Here am I, the servant of the Lord; let it be with me according to your word." Then the angel departed from her.

- Mary, the young girl of no status, from the village of Nazareth, an utterly insignificant place, is singled out, called, chosen, and overshadowed with God's Spirit. Her response moves from one of fear to total trust in God's inscrutable designs.

- "Mary has always been proposed to the faithful by the Church as an example to be imitated, not precisely in the type of life that she led and much less for the sociocultural background in which she lived and which scarcely exists anywhere today. Rather she is held up as an example to the faithful for the way in which in her own particular life she fully and responsibly accepted the word of God and acted on it, and because charity and the spirit of service were the driving force of her actions. She is worthy of imitation because she was the first and most perfect of Christ's disciples." (Pope Paul VI)

Wednesday December 9
Matthew 11:28–30

"Come to me, all you that are weary and are carrying heavy burdens, and I will give you rest. Take my yoke upon you, and learn from me; for I am gentle and humble in heart, and you will find rest for your souls. For my yoke is easy, and my burden is light."

- Here we see Jesus as the epitome of the Beatitudes for he presents himself as gentle and humble in heart. We see this in the way that throughout the Gospels he is comfortable with our limitations as human beings, and also in the way he invites us to face the greatness he shares with us.

- Be with Jesus for some time as he invites you to rest with these two sides of yourself that he wants you to live happily with. In doing this Jesus promises that you will find rest for your soul.

Thursday December 10
Matthew 11:11–15

"Truly I tell you, among those born of women no one has arisen greater than John the Baptist; yet the least in the kingdom of heaven is greater than he. From the days of John the Baptist until now the kingdom of heaven has suffered violence, and the violent take it by force. For all the prophets and the law prophesied until John came; and if you are willing to accept it, he is Elijah who is to come. Let anyone with ears listen!"

- John proclaimed the gospel, allowing his disciples to leave him to follow Jesus. I think of what it might mean to be less so that Jesus might be more.

- I ponder on what Jesus said about the greatness of John. I think of what he had seen and heard so that I might profit from understanding what Jesus valued.

Friday December 11
Matthew 11:16–19

"But to what will I compare this generation? It is
    like children sitting in the marketplaces and
    calling to one another,
'We played the flute for you, and you did not dance;
    we wailed, and you did not mourn.'

For John came neither eating nor drinking, and they say, 'He has a demon'; the Son of Man came eating and drinking, and they say, 'Look, a glutton and a drunkard, a friend of tax-collectors and sinners!' Yet wisdom is vindicated by her deeds."

- Matthew once again brings Jesus and John before us. There is a sense of dissatisfaction in the people. They are childish in their response! Neither one meets their demands or their criteria. Both cause the people to feel uncomfortable and disturbed. So they reject them out of hand.

- Lord, I recognize something of my own response to people here. I am not always open to listening and accepting those who are different. I can so easily judge, dismiss, and reject people. I need your help today.

Saturday December 12
Luke 1:26–38

In the sixth month the angel Gabriel was sent by God to a town in Galilee called Nazareth, to a virgin engaged to a man whose name was Joseph, of the house of David. The virgin's name was Mary. And he came to her and said, "Greetings, favored one! The Lord is with you." But she was much perplexed by his words and pondered what sort of greeting this might be. The angel said to her, "Do not be afraid, Mary, for you have found favor with God. And now, you will conceive in your womb and bear a son, and you will name him Jesus. He will be great, and will be called the Son of the Most High, and the Lord God will give to him the throne of his ancestor David. He will reign over the house of Jacob forever, and of his kingdom there will be no end." Mary said to the angel, "How can this be, since I am a virgin?" The angel said to her, "The Holy Spirit will come upon you, and the power of the Most High will overshadow you; therefore the child to be born will be holy; he will be called Son of God. And now, your relative Elizabeth in her old age has also conceived a son; and this is the sixth month for her who was said to be barren. For nothing will be impossible with God." Then Mary said, "Here am I, the servant of the Lord; let it be with me according to your word." Then the angel departed from her.

- The angel said to Mary, "You will conceive and bear a son," not "Are you willing to conceive and bear a son?" That is how God's will comes to us; sometimes in the things that happen to us, other times in what we choose, and often in a mixture of both.

- Nothing is impossible to God! In difficult times, it is good to remember that God is fully in charge of our world. Everything happens according to his plan. There is always hope.

The Third Week of Advent
December 13–19, 2020

Something to think and pray about each day this week:

We are more than halfway there. May God continue to guide the journey—the Advent trail for you and all.

Maybe we can spend a bit of time with those far distant travelers, the "wise" ones, on their journey (Matthew 2:1-12). We don't need to get too deeply involved in the history or the geography of it, apart from seeking directions, but let us acknowledge today their thirst for salvation and their search for the Savior.

With the best will in the world, they finished up in the wrong place. Herod's palace was certainly not the place to find the Messiah. Herod's world allowed neither space nor time for such wonderings. It was headquarters, and the feeling was there was no need to look anywhere else for power. This was the place from which you sought an appointment, the place you came to behold royalty and the trappings of power. Here you found servants and security, dancers and musicians, fools and sages, and maybe, above all, ego.

Into this place they came, seeking (as we do) to find the Messiah. The question threw Herod and his court into confusion. Advisers were brought in, people who knew the text but not its purpose, people who dealt in facts and not in faith, and they arrived at a consensus around where Christ was to be found. It was, for them and Herod, a destination, a spot on a map, but for the Wise Kings, it was neither—it was destiny, fulfillment of a promise, a dream come true. But all this was beyond Herod. The wise ones left the palace behind, the king in his confused glory, and realized the truth—that same truth we are seeking— that Christ lives among people, totally accessible for those who wish to come into his presence.

At times though, in our confusion, we might well continue to seek him in the wrong place.

Vincent Sherlock, *Let Advent Be Advent*
Messenger Publications, 2017

The Presence of God
At any time of the day or night we can call on Jesus.
He is always waiting, listening for our call.
What a wonderful blessing.
No phone needed, no e-mails, just a whisper.

Freedom
Lord, grant me the grace to have freedom of the spirit.
Cleanse my heart and soul so that I may live joyously
in your love.

Consciousness
Knowing that God loves me unconditionally, I look
honestly over the past day, its events, and my feelings.
Do I have something to be grateful for? Then I give
thanks. Is there something I am sorry for? Then I ask
forgiveness.

The Word
The word of God comes down to us through the
Scriptures.
May the Holy Spirit enlighten my mind and my heart
to respond to the Gospel teachings:
to love my neighbor as myself,
to care for my sisters and brothers in Christ.
(Please turn to the Scripture on the following pages.
Inspiration points are there, should you need them.
When you are ready, return here to continue.)

Conversation

I know with certainty that there were times when you carried me, Lord. There were times when it was through your strength that I got through the dark times in my life.

Conclusion

Glory be to the Father, and to the Son, and to the Holy Spirit,
As it was in the beginning, is now, and ever shall be,
World without end. Amen.

Sunday December 13
Third Sunday of Advent
John 1:6–8, 19–28

There was a man sent from God, whose name was John. He came as a witness to testify to the light, so that all might believe through him. He himself was not the light, but he came to testify to the light. . . .

This is the testimony given by John when the Jews sent priests and Levites from Jerusalem to ask him, "Who are you?" He confessed and did not deny it, but confessed, "I am not the Messiah." And they asked him, "What then? Are you Elijah?" He said, "I am not." "Are you the prophet?" He answered, "No." Then they said to him, "Who are you? Let us have an answer for those who sent us. What do you say about yourself?" He said, "I am the voice of one crying out in the wilderness, 'Make straight the way of the Lord,'" as the prophet Isaiah said.

Now they had been sent from the Pharisees. They asked him, "Why then are you baptizing if you are neither the Messiah, nor Elijah, nor the prophet?" John answered them, "I baptize with water. Among you stands one whom you do not know, the one who is coming after me; I am not worthy to untie the thong of his sandal." This took place in Bethany across the Jordan where John was baptizing.

- John knew that his role was to bring people to Christ. So is ours. We try to live our lives right so that people will be able to know through us that faith in Christ makes all the difference.

- John knew that his baptism was preparatory; it was only with water. Jesus baptized each of us with the Holy Spirit. The Holy Spirit dwells in us; he leads and guides us; we try to be open to his powerful work in our hearts.

Monday December 14
Matthew 21:23–27

When he entered the temple, the chief priests and the elders of the people came to him as he was teaching, and said, "By what authority are you doing these things, and who gave you this authority?" Jesus said to them, "I will also ask you one question; if you tell me the answer, then I will also tell you by what authority I do these things. Did the baptism of John come from heaven, or was it of human origin?" And they argued with one another, "If we say, 'From heaven,' he will say to us, 'Why then did you not believe him?' But if we say, 'Of human origin,' we are afraid of the crowd; for all regard John as a prophet." So they answered Jesus, "We do not know." And he said to them, "Neither will I tell you by what authority I am doing these things."

- Jesus was no stranger to the controversy and conflict of the religious establishment. They held a fixed view of how the Messiah should come. They demanded to know the source of his authority. He leaves them grappling in their stubbornness of heart.

- St. John of the Cross grappled with the mystery of who Jesus was. His life was spent contemplating the mystery of the Beloved. He wrote, "in the evening of life we will be examined in love." Lord, let me not seek to tame your word or curtail the Spirit. Rather keep me open today to holy mystery.

Tuesday December 15
Matthew 21:28–32

"What do you think? A man had two sons; he went to the first and said, 'Son, go and work in the vineyard today.' He answered, 'I will not'; but later he changed his mind and went. The father went to the second and said the same; and he answered, 'I go, sir'; but he did not go. Which of the two did the will of his father?" They said, "The first." Jesus said to them, "Truly I tell you, the tax-collectors and the prostitutes are going into the kingdom of God ahead of you. For John came to you in the way of righteousness and you did not believe him, but the tax-collectors and the prostitutes believed him; and even after you saw it, you did not change your minds and believe him."

- The Gospel reminds us of something we often forget: words can be meaningless. Promises are empty when not followed by action. The first son is arrogant, but his action shows his goodness. The second son sounds cooperative but fails to keep his promise.

- Do I make promises to others that quickly go out the window? My good intentions are no good to the person I intended to help but didn't. Could I say: "I'm sorry, I won't be able to do that for you," instead of promising what I already know is not going to happen?

- Let me take a few moments of silence to read over the Gospel text again and see if anything comes to my attention. And I could make a prayer, asking for help to be honest in speaking of my intentions.

Wednesday December 16

Luke 7:18b–23

John summoned two of his disciples and sent them to the Lord to ask, "Are you the one who is to come, or are we to wait for another?" When the men had come to him, they said, "John the Baptist has sent us to you to ask, 'Are you the one who is to come, or are we to wait for another?'" Jesus had just then cured many people of diseases, plagues, and evil spirits, and had given sight to many who were blind. And he answered them, "Go and tell John what you have seen and heard: the blind receive their sight, the lame walk, the lepers are cleansed, the deaf hear, the dead are raised, the poor have good news brought to them. And blessed is anyone who takes no offense at me."

- John has been tossed into prison. As he languishes there, the oil of his lamp is burning out. He wonders, did he get it right? Was his ministry a waste? Is Jesus the one he believed him to be?

- Lord, I can identify with John. I too find the wick of my lamp can sputter, the flame quiver, when things don't go my way. My desire for a world of peace and justice is met by a world of violence and injustice. This Advent day, refill my inner lamp and let me walk in faith and trust.

Thursday December 17
Matthew 1:1–17

An account of the genealogy of Jesus the Messiah, the son of David, the son of Abraham.

Abraham was the father of Isaac, and Isaac the father of Jacob, and Jacob the father of Judah and his brothers, and Judah the father of Perez and Zerah by Tamar, and Perez the father of Hezron, and Hezron the father of Aram, and Aram the father of Aminadab, and Aminadab the father of Nahshon, and Nahshon the father of Salmon, and Salmon the father of Boaz by Rahab, and Boaz the father of Obed by Ruth, and Obed the father of Jesse, and Jesse the father of King David.

And David was the father of Solomon by the wife of Uriah, and Solomon the father of Rehoboam, and Rehoboam the father of Abijah, and Abijah the father of Asaph, and Asaph the father of Jehoshaphat, and Jehoshaphat the father of Joram, and Joram the father of Uzziah, and Uzziah the father of Jotham, and Jotham the father of Ahaz, and Ahaz the father of Hezekiah, and Hezekiah the father of Manasseh, and Manasseh the father of Amos, and Amos the father of Josiah, and Josiah the father of Jechoniah and his brothers, at the time of the deportation to Babylon.

And after the deportation to Babylon: Jechoniah was the father of Salathiel, and Salathiel the father of Zerubbabel, and Zerubbabel the father of Abiud, and Abiud the father of Eliakim, and Eliakim the father of Azor, and Azor the father of Zadok, and Zadok the father of Achim, and Achim the father of Eliud, and Eliud the father of Eleazar, and Eleazar the father of Matthan, and Matthan the father of Jacob, and Jacob the father of Joseph the husband of Mary, of whom Jesus was born, who is called the Messiah.

So all the generations from Abraham to David are fourteen generations; and from David to the deportation to Babylon, fourteen generations; and from the deportation to Babylon to the Messiah, fourteen generations.

- There are surprises in this list of Jesus' ancestors. Matthew's genealogy is revolutionary for his time, in that it features five women. In addition, four of the women were Gentiles. Add to that the presence of some notable sinners, such as Judah and King David, and the intention is clear. It is to highlight the inclusivity of Jesus' mission.

- Paul says in Galatians 3:28–29: "There is neither Jew nor Gentile, neither slave nor free, nor is there male and female, for you are all one in Christ Jesus. If you belong to Christ, then you are Abraham's seed, and heirs according to the promise."

Friday December 18
Matthew 1:18–25

Now the birth of Jesus the Messiah took place in this way. When his mother Mary had been engaged to Joseph, but before they lived together, she was found to be with child from the Holy Spirit. Her husband Joseph, being a righteous man and unwilling to expose her to public disgrace, planned to dismiss her quietly. But just when he had resolved to do this, an angel of the Lord appeared to him in a dream and said, "Joseph, son of David, do not be afraid to take Mary as your wife, for the child conceived in her is from the Holy Spirit. She will bear a son, and you are to name him Jesus, for he will save his people from their sins." All this took place to fulfill what had been spoken by the Lord through the prophet: "Look, the virgin shall conceive and bear a son, and they shall name him Emmanuel," which means, "God is with us." When Joseph awoke from sleep, he did as the angel of the Lord commanded him; he took her as his wife, but had no marital relations with her until she had borne a son; and he named him Jesus.

- The Spirit (or Breath) of God was seen as the source of all creation and of all human life. So, just as God created all that exists in the heavens and the earth, now, through the power of God's Spirit, Jesus is conceived in Mary's womb by a particular, concrete, and special case of God's creativity.

- The birth of any child brings with it a sense of awe and wonderment. Can I share a sense of awe and wonderment at the incredible fact that God becomes human in a baby boy?

Saturday December 19
Luke 1:5–25

In the days of King Herod of Judea, there was a priest named Zechariah, who belonged to the priestly order of Abijah. His wife was a descendant of Aaron, and her name was Elizabeth. Both of them were righteous before God, living blamelessly according to all the commandments and regulations of the Lord. But they had no children, because Elizabeth was barren, and both were getting on in years.

Once when he was serving as priest before God and his section was on duty, he was chosen by lot, according to the custom of the priesthood, to enter the sanctuary of the Lord and offer incense. Now at the time of the incense offering, the whole assembly of the people was praying outside. Then there appeared to him an angel of the Lord, standing at the right side of the altar of incense. When Zechariah saw him, he was terrified; and fear overwhelmed him. But the angel said to him, "Do not be afraid, Zechariah, for your prayer has been heard. Your wife Elizabeth will bear you a son, and you will name him John. You will have joy and gladness, and many will rejoice at his birth, for he will be great in the sight of the Lord. He must never drink wine or strong drink; even before his birth he will be filled with the Holy Spirit. He will turn many of the people of Israel to the Lord their God. With the spirit and power of Elijah he will go before him, to turn the hearts of parents to their children, and the disobedient to the wisdom of the righteous, to make ready a people prepared for the Lord." Zechariah said to the angel, "How will I know that this is so? For I am an old man, and my wife is getting on in years." The angel replied, "I am Gabriel. I stand in the presence of God, and I have been sent to speak to you and to bring you this good news. But now, because you did not believe my words, which will be fulfilled in their time, you will become mute, unable to speak, until the day these things occur."

Meanwhile, the people were waiting for Zechariah, and wondered at his delay in the sanctuary. When he did come out, he could not speak to them, and they realized that he had seen a vision in the sanctuary. He kept motioning to them and remained unable to speak. When his time of service was ended, he went to his home.

After those days his wife Elizabeth conceived, and for five months she remained in seclusion. She said, "This is what the Lord has done for me when he looked favorably on me and took away the disgrace I have endured among my people."

- Elizabeth was barren and God intervened to show his power. Where is my life barren, empty? Where do I want God to intervene for me?

- Zechariah doubted the angel's message and was punished for it. I ask for God's help with my own doubts and difficulties.

December 20–26, 2020

Something to think and pray about each day this week:

They walk to the back of their home
The shed is alive . . . .
Shepherd boys
A young drummer
A smiling mother
Others, they're told, on the way.

The animals there too
Breathing warmth on one so new
The man who had knocked and asked for a bed
The one that was almost sent on his way
But then—the change of heart
The shed was offered
The right thing to do of course
Especially when they saw the young woman
A breath away from giving birth to new breath
How could you leave them in the cold?
The two of them there now
No longer two but three
On bended knee
He looked at his Infant guest
Thankful he'd done his best
And walked back to the house

She looked at him
And smiled
"Now," she said
"aren't you glad you cleaned the shed?"
He was.
We are.

It was the only way to prepare . . . .
To clean
Be clean
Fit for a King.
Amen!

Vincent Sherlock, *Let Advent be Advent*
Messenger Publications, 2017

The Presence of God
As I sit here, the beating of my heart,
the ebb and flow of my breathing, the movements of
my mind
are all signs of God's ongoing creation of me.
I pause for a moment and become aware
of this presence of God within me.

Freedom
It is so easy to get caught up
with the trappings of wealth in this life.
Grant, O Lord, that I may be free
from greed and selfishness.
Remind me that the best things in life are free:
Love, laughter, caring, and sharing.

Consciousness
Knowing that God loves me unconditionally, I can
afford to be honest about how I am.
How has the day been, and how do I feel now? I share
my feelings openly with the Lord.

The Word
Lord Jesus, you became human to communicate with
me.
You walked and worked on this earth.
You endured the heat and struggled with the cold.
All your time on this earth was spent in caring for
humanity.

You healed the sick, you raised the dead.
Most important of all, you saved me from death.
(Please turn to the Scripture on the following pages.
Inspiration points are there, should you need them.
When you are ready, return here to continue.)

Conversation
Sometimes I wonder what I might say if I were to meet you in person, Lord.
I think I might say, "Thank you" because you are always there for me.

Conclusion
I thank God for these moments we have spent together and for any insights I have been given concerning the text.

Sunday December 20
Fourth Sunday of Advent

Luke 1:26–38

In the sixth month the angel Gabriel was sent by God to a town in Galilee called Nazareth, to a virgin engaged to a man whose name was Joseph, of the house of David. The virgin's name was Mary. And he came to her and said, "Greetings, favored one! The Lord is with you." But she was much perplexed by his words and pondered what sort of greeting this might be. The angel said to her, "Do not be afraid, Mary, for you have found favor with God. And now, you will conceive in your womb and bear a son, and you will name him Jesus. He will be great, and will be called the Son of the Most High, and the Lord God will give to him the throne of his ancestor David. He will reign over the house of Jacob forever, and of his kingdom there will be no end." Mary said to the angel, "How can this be, since I am a virgin?" The angel said to her, "The Holy Spirit will come upon you, and the power of the Most High will overshadow you; therefore the child to be born will be holy; he will be called Son of God. And now, your relative Elizabeth in her old age has also conceived a son; and this is the sixth month for her who was said to be barren. For nothing will be impossible with God." Then Mary said, "Here am I, the servant of the Lord; let it be with me according to your word." Then the angel departed from her.

- Theologians constructed a theory of original sin, and another theory to explain how Mary was exempt from the curse of Adam: the Immaculate Conception. In prayer I'd rather remember the old Irish poem:

> Queen of all queens, oh wonder of the loveliness
>   of women,
> Heart which hath held in check for us the
>   righteous wrath of God;
> Strong staff of light and fosterer of the Bright
>   Child of heaven,
> Pray thou for us as we now pray that we may be
>   forgiven.

- Repeating a phrase in prayer may make it go deep within us. It's like a favorite piece of music that we can hum over and over again. It is part of us. "I am the servant of the Lord" was such a phrase for Mary, spoken first at one of the biggest moments in her life. In dry times of prayer, a sentence like that can occupy mind and heart and raise us close to God.

Monday December 21
Luke 1:39–45

In those days Mary set out and went with haste to a Judean town in the hill country, where she entered the house of Zechariah and greeted Elizabeth. When Elizabeth heard Mary's greeting, the child leaped in her womb. And Elizabeth was filled with the Holy Spirit and exclaimed with a loud cry, "Blessed are you among women, and blessed is the fruit of your womb. And why has this happened to me, that the mother of my Lord comes to me? For as soon as I heard the sound of your greeting, the child in my womb leaped for joy. And blessed is she who believed that there would be a fulfillment of what was spoken to her by the Lord."

- Birth, the gift of life from God, fruitfulness was always sacred to the people of Israel; and the mothers had a special place down through sacred history—as the bearers of life. Mary and Elizabeth outdo one another, as it were, in giving thanks.

- But this particular case is special, unique. Jesus, the child that Mary is carrying, is recognized by the child in Elizabeth's womb—John leaps in recognition of the one whom both mothers revere as "Lord" (John himself being of miraculous origin from an elderly mother).

- And above and beyond what is happening to each mother, earthshaking events are in store; the Lord (long awaited) has finally come to visit his people, to be victorious over enemies, to exult with joy over those who are his own.

Tuesday December 22
Luke 1:46–56
And Mary said,
"My soul magnifies the Lord,

and my spirit rejoices in God my Savior, for he has
looked with favor on the lowliness of his servant.
Surely, from now on all generations will call
    me blessed;
for the Mighty One has done great things for me,
    and holy is his name.
His mercy is for those who fear him
    from generation to generation.
He has shown strength with his arm;
    he has scattered the proud in the thoughts of
        their hearts.
He has brought down the powerful from their thrones,
    and lifted up the lowly;
he has filled the hungry with good things,
    and sent the rich away empty.
He has helped his servant Israel,
    in remembrance of his mercy,
according to the promise he made to our ancestors,
    to Abraham and to his descendants for ever."

And Mary remained with her for about three months
and then returned to her home.

- This glorious prayer, the Magnificat, is charged with dynamite. It points to a society in which nobody wants to have too much while others have too little. The hungry are fed and the lowly are raised up.

- Lord, may I never be seduced by sweet devotion while I have more than I need and others have less.

Wednesday December 23

Luke 1:57–66

Now the time came for Elizabeth to give birth, and she bore a son. Her neighbors and relatives heard that the Lord had shown his great mercy to her, and they rejoiced with her.

On the eighth day they came to circumcise the child, and they were going to name him Zechariah after his father. But his mother said, "No; he is to be called John." They said to her, "None of your relatives has this name." Then they began motioning to his father to find out what name he wanted to give him. He asked for a writing tablet and wrote, "His name is John." And all of them were amazed. Immediately his mouth was opened and his tongue freed, and he began to speak, praising God. Fear came over all their neighbors, and all these things were talked about throughout the entire hill country of Judea. All who heard them pondered them and said, "What then will this child become?" For, indeed, the hand of the Lord was with him.

- The neighbors and relatives who attended the circumcision had their well-worn expectation about the child's name. But they had to learn that it is God who chooses the name and the destiny of this child. Perhaps, with every child, God moves the world in a new direction?

- How do I stay open to the God of surprises, to the Spirit who moves at will? Is my comfort zone too well defended for me to be surprised by grace?

Thursday December 24

Luke 1:67–79

Then his father Zechariah was filled with the Holy
Spirit and spoke this prophecy:

"Blessed be the Lord God of Israel,
>   for he has looked favorably on his people and
>   redeemed them.

He has raised up a mighty savior for us
>   in the house of his servant David,

as he spoke through the mouth of his holy prophets
>   from of old,

>   that we would be saved from our enemies and
>   from the hand of all who hate us.

Thus he has shown the mercy promised to our
>   ancestors,

>   and has remembered his holy covenant,

the oath that he swore to our ancestor Abraham,
>   to grant us that we, being rescued from the
>   hands of our enemies,

might serve him without fear, in holiness and
>   righteousness

>   before him all our days.

And you, child, will be called the prophet of the
>   Most High;

>   for you will go before the Lord to prepare his ways,

to give knowledge of salvation to his people
>   by the forgiveness of their sins.

By the tender mercy of our God,
>   the dawn from on high will break upon us,

to give light to those who sit in darkness and in the
   shadow of death,
      to guide our feet into the way of peace."

- Zechariah, released from his silence, bursts forth in
  profound praise, proclaiming the activity of God at
  work in our world's history. The savior is coming! His
  own son will act as witness and light-bearer to the
  lovingkindness and mercy of the great and holy one.

- Lord, as I move into Christmas Eve, remind me
  again of how mercy is the dominant theme of how
  you walk with us. You are forever tender toward
  me. Help me to grow daily in the awareness of your
  mercy and tenderness, constantly at work in my life.

Friday December 25
The Nativity of the Lord
John 1:1–18

In the beginning was the Word, and the Word was
with God, and the Word was God. He was in the beginning with God. All things came into being through
him, and without him not one thing came into being.
What has come into being in him was life, and the
life was the light of all people. The light shines in the
darkness, and the darkness did not overcome it.

   There was a man sent from God, whose name was
John. He came as a witness to testify to the light, so that
all might believe through him. He himself was not the

light, but he came to testify to the light. The true light, which enlightens everyone, was coming into the world.

He was in the world, and the world came into being through him; yet the world did not know him. He came to what was his own, and his own people did not accept him. But to all who received him, who believed in his name, he gave power to become children of God, who were born, not of blood or of the will of the flesh or of the will of man, but of God.

And the Word became flesh and lived among us, and we have seen his glory, the glory as of a father's only son, full of grace and truth. (John testified to him and cried out, "This was he of whom I said, 'He who comes after me ranks ahead of me because he was before me.'") From his fullness we have all received, grace upon grace. The law indeed was given through Moses; grace and truth came through Jesus Christ. No one has ever seen God. It is God the only Son, who is close to the Father's heart, who has made him known.

- This is the "Christmas Gospel." Christmas is not simply the celebration of the birth of the baby Jesus but also the awesome mystery of the Incarnation of God. God pitched his tent among us and remains among us as a human being forever.

- The world did not know him. His own people, the leaders of the Jews, did not accept him. We have accepted him, and our vocation is to make his light shine for the whole world.

Saturday December 26
St. Stephen, Martyr

Matthew 10:17–22

Beware of them, for they will hand you over to councils and flog you in their synagogues; and you will be dragged before governors and kings because of me, as a testimony to them and the Gentiles. When they hand you over, do not worry about how you are to speak or what you are to say; for what you are to say will be given to you at that time; for it is not you who speak, but the Spirit of your Father speaking through you. Brother will betray brother to death, and a father his child, and children will rise against parents and have them put to death; and you will be hated by all because of my name. But the one who endures to the end will be saved.

- It can seem strange to celebrate St. Stephen, who was martyred, right after Christmas Day when our dominant emotion is joy in the birth of Christ. The point, however, is that this is why Christ came to earth, to save us from our sins by his death on the cross.

- Christian joy is that strange thing, not an emotion, but a deep peace that remains even in the midst of great opposition and difficulty. This will always be part of the Christian life.

December 27, 2020–January 2, 2021

Something to think and pray about each day this week:

He was every inch of what you'd expect a wise man to be. Tall, ponderous, intuitive and generous with those who weren't wasting his time. His professional life was lived as a professor of sociology and a priest. He lived through the horrors of the Rwandan genocide and he lives through it still as he endeavors to reason with the tremendous evils he witnessed. I can still hear the quiver in his voice when, twenty years after the genocide, he said, "You know that humanity has crossed a line when fathers can murder their own children." In truth he saw the slaughter of many innocents. He paused and said nothing for quite a while.

A few weeks later I was reading up on the genocide. The author, another priest, said that "tribal identities became more important than baptismal identity." Either we are all the same as children of God and we demand to both give and receive mutual respect, or we create tribes where we make ourselves more important or more valuable than others who occupy the same space.

Alan Hilliard, *Dipping into Advent*
Messenger Publications, 2019

The Presence of God

"Be still, and know that I am God!" Lord, your words lead us to the calmness and greatness of your presence.

Freedom

If God were trying to tell me something, would I know?

If God were reassuring me or challenging me, would I notice?

I ask for the grace to be free of my own preoccupations and open to what God may be saying to me.

Consciousness

In the presence of my loving Creator, I look honestly at my feelings over the past day: the highs, the lows, and the level ground. Can I see where the Lord has been present?

The Word

In this expectant state of mind, please turn to the text for the day with confidence. Believe that the Holy Spirit is present and may reveal whatever the passage has to say to you. Read reflectively, listening with a third ear to what may be going on in your heart. (Please turn to the Scripture on the following pages. Inspiration points are there, should you need them. When you are ready, return here to continue.)

Conversation

Remembering that I am still in God's presence,
I imagine Jesus standing or sitting beside me,
and I say whatever is on my mind, whatever is in my heart,
speaking as one friend to another.

Conclusion

Glory be to the Father, and to the Son, and to the Holy Spirit,
As it was in the beginning, is now, and ever shall be,
World without end. Amen.

Sunday December 27
The Holy Family of Jesus, Mary and Joseph
Luke 2:22–40

When the time came for their purification according to the law of Moses, they brought him up to Jerusalem to present him to the Lord (as it is written in the law of the Lord, "Every firstborn male shall be designated as holy to the Lord"), and they offered a sacrifice according to what is stated in the law of the Lord, "a pair of turtledoves or two young pigeons."

Now there was a man in Jerusalem whose name was Simeon; this man was righteous and devout, looking forward to the consolation of Israel, and the Holy Spirit rested on him. It had been revealed to him by the Holy Spirit that he would not see death before he had seen the Lord's Messiah. Guided by the Spirit, Simeon came into the temple; and when the parents brought in the child Jesus, to do for him what was customary under the law, Simeon took him in his arms and praised God, saying,

"Master, now you are dismissing your servant in
      peace,
      according to your word;
for my eyes have seen your salvation,
      which you have prepared in the presence of all
         peoples,

a light for revelation to the Gentiles
    and for glory to your people Israel."

And the child's father and mother were amazed at what was being said about him. Then Simeon blessed them and said to his mother Mary, "This child is destined for the falling and the rising of many in Israel, and to be a sign that will be opposed so that the inner thoughts of many will be revealed—and a sword will pierce your own soul too."

There was also a prophet, Anna the daughter of Phanuel, of the tribe of Asher. She was of a great age, having lived with her husband for seven years after her marriage, then as a widow to the age of eighty-four. She never left the temple but worshiped there with fasting and prayer night and day. At that moment she came, and began to praise God and to speak about the child to all who were looking for the redemption of Jerusalem.

When they had finished everything required by the law of the Lord, they returned to Galilee, to their own town of Nazareth. The child grew and became strong, filled with wisdom; and the favor of God was upon him.

• The Holy Spirit is very important for St. Luke, and that Spirit is never far away. This text links him closely to Simeon, helping the old man to recognize and praise God, and to bless the parents of Jesus. What about me? The Holy Spirit dwells in me too: I am his temple! But is he perhaps only a quiet lodger whom I hardly notice? Have I locked him up? Can he become my mentor whom I look to for advice and support? Can the Spirit and I create life together?

- The early Christians announced important decisions by saying, "It has seemed good to the Holy Spirit and to us . . ." (Acts 15:28). Lord, make me sensitive to the Spirit's promptings as I make my decisions. Then things will go well for me.

Monday December 28
The Holy Innocents
Matthew 2:13–18

Now after they had left, an angel of the Lord appeared to Joseph in a dream and said, "Get up, take the child and his mother, and flee to Egypt, and remain there until I tell you; for Herod is about to search for the child, to destroy him." Then Joseph got up, took the child and his mother by night, and went to Egypt, and remained there until the death of Herod. This was to fulfill what had been spoken by the Lord through the prophet, "Out of Egypt I have called my son."

When Herod saw that he had been tricked by the wise men, he was infuriated, and he sent and killed all the children in and around Bethlehem who were two years old or under, according to the time that he had learned from the wise men. Then was fulfilled what had been spoken through the prophet Jeremiah:

"A voice was heard in Ramah,
    wailing and loud lamentation,
Rachel weeping for her children;
    she refused to be consoled, because they are no
        more."

- Another sad feast, remembering Herod's blood-thirsty massacre and the heartbreak of the babies' mothers. As we recover from Christmas, other parts of the world—even of our own country—are suffering bombs, bloodshed, bereavements. Lord, keep my heart open to the griefs that confront me.

- This terrible scene evokes the genocides and atrocities that still make the news. I pray with compassion for all who are affected by violence and cruelty.

- Herod's action was motivated by his pride and self-seeking. As I pray for all leaders, I ask God to heal me of any false image I have of myself.

Tuesday December 29
Luke 2:22–35

When the time came for their purification according to the law of Moses, they brought him up to Jerusalem to present him to the Lord (as it is written in the law of the Lord, "Every firstborn male shall be designated as holy to the Lord"), and they offered a sacrifice according to what is stated in the law of the Lord, "a pair of turtledoves or two young pigeons."

Now there was a man in Jerusalem whose name was Simeon; this man was righteous and devout, looking forward to the consolation of Israel, and the Holy Spirit rested on him. It had been revealed to him by the Holy Spirit that he would not see death before he had seen the Lord's Messiah. Guided by the Spirit, Simeon came into the temple; and when the parents brought in the child Jesus, to do for him what was customary under the law, Simeon took him in his arms and praised God, saying,

"Master, now you are dismissing your servant in peace,
     according to your word;
for my eyes have seen your salvation,
     which you have prepared in the presence of all
          peoples,
a light for revelation to the Gentiles
     and for glory to your people Israel."

And the child's father and mother were amazed at what was being said about him. Then Simeon blessed them and said to his mother Mary, "This child is destined for the falling and the rising of many in Israel, and to be a sign that will be opposed so that the inner thoughts of many will be revealed—and a sword will pierce your own soul too."

- Simeon was one of those known as The Quiet in the Land, Jews who did not look for a military Messiah, and had no dreams of armies or power, but believed in a life of constant watchfulness and prayer until God should come. There is a double surprise here: the delight of Simeon at being able to welcome the Promised One; and the astonishment of Mary and Joseph at what was being said about their boy.

• Lord, may I too open my eyes in grateful amazement when I see your interventions in my life.

Wednesday December 30
Luke 2:36–40

There was also a prophet, Anna the daughter of Phanuel, of the tribe of Asher. She was of a great age, having lived with her husband for seven years after her marriage, then as a widow to the age of eighty-four. She never left the temple but worshiped there with fasting and prayer night and day. At that moment she came, and began to praise God and to speak about the child to all who were looking for the redemption of Jerusalem.

When they had finished everything required by the law of the Lord, they returned to Galilee, to their own town of Nazareth. The child grew and became strong, filled with wisdom; and the favor of God was upon him.

• The redemption of Jerusalem was such a long time coming, so many centuries. Think how many old women in Israel looked forward in vain over all those years. How blessed was Anna that she saw the Savior just before she died. Think how blessed we are to have the Savior near us every day of our lives.

- Jesus spent thirty of his thirty-three years on earth living an ordinary life with his parents in Nazareth. These "hidden years" reveal to us the fundamental value of our ordinary day-to-day lives. Every day is crucial, with such richness and potential, which we need to consider seriously.

Thursday December 31
John 1:1–18

In the beginning was the Word, and the Word was with God, and the Word was God. He was in the beginning with God. All things came into being through him, and without him not one thing came into being. What has come into being in him was life, and the life was the light of all people. The light shines in the darkness, and the darkness did not overcome it.

There was a man sent from God, whose name was John. He came as a witness to testify to the light, so that all might believe through him. He himself was not the light, but he came to testify to the light. The true light, which enlightens everyone, was coming into the world.

He was in the world, and the world came into being through him; yet the world did not know him. He came to what was his own, and his own people did not accept him. But to all who received him, who believed in his name, he gave power to become children of God, who were born, not of blood or of the will of the flesh or of the will of man, but of God.

And the Word became flesh and lived among us, and we have seen his glory, the glory as of a father's only son, full of grace and truth. (John testified to him and cried out, "This was he of whom I said, 'He who comes after me ranks ahead of me because he was before me.'") From his fullness we have all received, grace upon grace. The law indeed was given through Moses; grace and truth came through Jesus Christ. No one has ever seen God. It is God the only Son, who is close to the Father's heart, who has made him known.

- As our year draws to a close, today's Scripture brings us back to the beginning of all time. As we stand on the threshold of another year, we take time to recall the greatest event of all: God has entered our world, not just for a day's visit, but has made it his permanent dwelling.

- Lord, let me set aside some time today, to reflect back on how the light of your presence has impacted my life during this past year. Let me be grateful and give thanks for all I have received from you directly and through the gift of other people.

Friday January 1
Mary the Mother of God
Luke 2:16–21

So they went with haste and found Mary and Joseph, and the child lying in the manger. When they saw this, they made known what had been told them about this child; and all who heard it were amazed at what the shepherds told them. But Mary treasured all these words and pondered them in her heart. The shepherds returned, glorifying and praising God for all they had heard and seen, as it had been told them.

After eight days had passed, it was time to circumcise the child; and he was called Jesus, the name given by the angel before he was conceived in the womb.

- This is the octave day of Christmas, dedicated as a solemnity to Mary, the Holy Mother of God. The Gospel invites us to join the shepherds as they visit the newborn child in Bethlehem, and to share in their wonder and joy. Have our celebrations over the Christmas season brought us closer to Jesus and his mother? Or have we found it difficult to find oases of quiet time in which to enter deeply into the mystery of it all?

- We cannot but be aware that this is also New Year's Day. How do we feel about entering a new phase of our journey through life? Are we in an expectant and hopeful mood, or are we apathetic or despondent? Whatever our feelings may be, it would be good to share them with God and ask his blessing on the days and months ahead.

Saturday January 2
John 1:19–28

This is the testimony given by John when the Jews sent priests and Levites from Jerusalem to ask him,

"Who are you?" He confessed and did not deny it, but confessed, "I am not the Messiah." And they asked him, "What then? Are you Elijah?" He said, "I am not." "Are you the prophet?" He answered, "No." Then they said to him, "Who are you? Let us have an answer for those who sent us. What do you say about yourself?" He said, "I am the voice of one crying out in the wilderness, 'Make straight the way of the Lord,'" as the prophet Isaiah said.

Now they had been sent from the Pharisees. They asked him, "Why then are you baptizing if you are neither the Messiah, nor Elijah, nor the prophet?" John answered them, "I baptize with water. Among you stands one whom you do not know, the one who is coming after me; I am not worthy to untie the thong of his sandal." This took place in Bethany across the Jordan where John was baptizing.

- "Who are you?" I put labels on people and think I know them. But can I even fathom the mystery of my own being? I cannot put an easy label on John the Baptist. He is a voice in the stillness of the desert. He points beyond himself. He doesn't want to be an achiever. May he stir up in me a longing to look for the One who is coming.

- Loving Father, who are you? I see in Jesus that you are pure gift of everlasting love. You are Mystery, beyond me. But in you I know my real worth and the value of everyone and everything in my life.

The Epiphany of Our Lord/
The Second Week of Christmas
January 3–10, 2021

Something to think and pray about each day this week:

Driving home one evening, I was enthralled by a radio documentary which related recordings of the last place in Ireland to receive electricity, or the "lectric," as it was called in the local dialect. The location was aptly called The Black Valley in County Kerry.

The producers went ahead of the installation and interviewed people who were full of frightened expectation as the cables made their way closer and closer to the last door in the country to receive this new form of power. An elderly couple were in the last house on the road and, being a proud homeowner, all she was worried about was having a clean house to welcome their new guest who promised to transform their lives. As the presenter talked, you could hear her scrubbing, moving, washing, and replacing over and over again. The familiar sound of a tin pail full of water and a mop sloshing around a stone floor only served to increase the sense of excited anticipation.

When the "lectric" was eventually installed, the switch in the house was flicked and, lo and behold, despite all the cleaning and polishing the brazen "lectric" bulb revealed dirt, cobwebs, and dust in places they didn't even know existed in their humble abode. There was utter embarrassment and discomfort all round.

We don't see light, but light helps us see. The opening of St. John's Gospel is called the prologue, and it tells us that Jesus is the "light that shines in the darkness and the darkness has not overcome it." He is described as the light because his ways, insights, and teachings help us see the world and our existence in a refreshingly unlimited manner. Sometimes his light, like the "lectric," may also show us where we have to tidy up our lives!

Alan Hilliard, *Dipping into Advent*
Messenger Publications, 2019

The Presence of God

"I am standing at the door, knocking," says the Lord. What a wonderful privilege that the Lord of all creation desires to come to me. I welcome his presence.

Freedom

I will ask God's help
to be free from my own preoccupations,
to be open to God in this time of prayer,
to come to know, love, and serve God more.

Consciousness

In God's loving presence I unwind the past day, starting from now and looking back, moment by moment.
I gather in all the goodness and light, in gratitude.
I attend to the shadows and what they say to me, seeking healing, courage, forgiveness.

The Word

Now I turn to the Scripture set out for me this day. I read slowly over the words and see if any sentence or sentiment appeals to me. (Please turn to the Scripture on the following pages. Inspiration points are there, should you need them. When you are ready, return here to continue.)

Conversation

Sometimes I wonder what I might say if I were to meet you in person, Lord.

I think I might say, "Thank you" because you are always there for me.

Conclusion

I thank God for these moments we have spent together and for any insights I have been given concerning the text.

Sunday January 3
Epiphany of the Lord (USA)
Matthew 2:1–12

In the time of King Herod, after Jesus was born in Bethlehem of Judea, wise men from the East came to Jerusalem, asking, "Where is the child who has been born king of the Jews? For we observed his star at its rising, and have come to pay him homage." When King Herod heard this, he was frightened, and all Jerusalem with him; and calling together all the chief priests and scribes of the people, he inquired of them where the Messiah was to be born. They told him, "In Bethlehem of Judea; for so it has been written by the prophet:

'And you, Bethlehem, in the land of Judah,
    are by no means least among the rulers of Judah;
for from you shall come a ruler
    who is to shepherd my people Israel.'"

Then Herod secretly called for the wise men and learned from them the exact time when the star had appeared. Then he sent them to Bethlehem, saying, "Go and search diligently for the child; and when you have found him, bring me word so that I may also go and pay him homage." When they had heard the king, they set out; and there, ahead of them, went the star that they had seen at its rising, until it stopped over the place where the child was. When they saw that the star had stopped, they were overwhelmed with joy. On entering the house, they saw the child with Mary his mother; and they knelt down and paid him homage. Then, opening their treasure chests, they offered him gifts of gold, frankincense, and myrrh. And having been warned in a dream not to return to Herod, they left for their own country by another road.

- The story told in today's Gospel is about people being called to follow their star in order to find the fullness of life only Jesus can give. "I came that they may have life, and have it abundantly" (John 10:10). You may not have thought much about the nature of the star you follow. With a view to clarifying this, it may be worthwhile to ask yourself what you want for your children, your family, or your friends.

- Having done this, you might talk to Jesus about whether this is what he wants for you, the star he wishes you to follow.

Monday January 4
Matthew 4:12–17, 23–25

Now when Jesus heard that John had been arrested, he withdrew to Galilee. He left Nazareth and made his home in Capernaum by the lake, in the territory of Zebulun and Naphtali, so that what had been spoken through the prophet Isaiah might be fulfilled:

"Land of Zebulun, land of Naphtali,
    on the road by the sea, across the Jordan,
    Galilee of the Gentiles—

the people who sat in darkness
    have seen a great light,
and for those who sat in the region and shadow of
    death
    light has dawned."
From that time Jesus began to proclaim, "Repent,
    for the kingdom of heaven has come near." . . .

Jesus went throughout Galilee, teaching in their synagogues and proclaiming the good news of the kingdom and curing every disease and every sickness among the people. So his fame spread throughout all Syria, and they brought to him all the sick, those who were afflicted with various diseases and pains, demoniacs, epileptics, and paralytics, and he cured them. And great crowds followed him from Galilee, the Decapolis, Jerusalem, Judea, and from beyond the Jordan.

• Here we are at the beginning of Jesus' ministry. He leaves Nazareth and settles in Capernaum, a busy fishing and trading center on the Sea of Galilee. His call to repentance is identical to that of John the Baptist.

• He is a late starter, a young man in a hurry. His hero, John, has been imprisoned, and he realizes his time may be short. He ministers to large crowds, proclaiming the Good News of the reign of God, healing all kinds of sickness and exorcising demons.

• Do I catch the excitement and enthusiasm of the crowds, come from far and wide?

Tuesday January 5
Mark 6:34–44

As he went ashore, he saw a great crowd; and he had compassion for them, because they were like sheep without a shepherd; and he began to teach them many things. When it grew late, his disciples came to him and said, "This is a deserted place, and the hour is now very late; send them away so that they may go into the surrounding country and villages and buy something for themselves to eat." But he answered them, "You give them something to eat." They said to him, "Are we to go and buy two hundred denarii worth of bread, and give it to them to eat?" And he said to them, "How many loaves have you? Go and see." When they had found out, they said, "Five, and two fish." Then he ordered them to get all the people to sit down in groups on the green grass. So they sat down in groups of hundreds and of fifties. Taking the five loaves and the two fish, he looked up to heaven, and blessed and broke the loaves, and gave them to his disciples to set before the people; and he divided the two fish among them all. And all ate and were filled; and they took up twelve baskets full of broken pieces and of the fish. Those who had eaten the loaves numbered five thousand men.

- The people of God had always looked forward to the coming of the Messiah or Savior—who would usher in an era of plenty with a feast for God's family. And this is what Jesus here provides.

- We are fortunate to be living in this golden age, when God—in Jesus—is ready to shower abundance upon us. We thank him for his gifts.

Wednesday January 6
Mark 6:45–52

Immediately he made his disciples get into the boat and go on ahead to the other side, to Bethsaida, while he dismissed the crowd. After saying farewell to them, he went up on the mountain to pray.

When evening came, the boat was out on the lake, and he was alone on the land. When he saw that they were straining at the oars against an adverse wind, he came towards them early in the morning, walking on the lake. He intended to pass them by. But when they saw him walking on the lake, they thought it was a ghost and cried out; for they all saw him and were terrified. But immediately he spoke to them and said, "Take heart, it is I; do not be afraid." Then he got into the boat with them and the wind ceased. And they were utterly astounded, for they did not understand about the loaves, but their hearts were hardened.

- Jesus is praying—speaking with his Father. Is he perhaps thinking about the best way to get through to people regarding what his coming is really about? Is he perhaps recalling the great demonstration that was his feeding of the five thousand? However in the minds of the people, that was seen only as the beginning of a political campaign. And the disciples were little better. So now he is about to intervene on a different level: he saves the disciples from the storm simply to show that he himself is strong enough for his cause to succeed without having to rely on the popular mood.

- Jesus is strong enough to carry out his plan for my life, without having to rely on people who "have influence."

Thursday January 7
Luke 4:14–22a

Then Jesus, filled with the power of the Spirit, returned to Galilee, and a report about him spread through all the surrounding country. He began to teach in their synagogues and was praised by everyone.

When he came to Nazareth, where he had been brought up, he went to the synagogue on the sabbath day, as was his custom. He stood up to read, and the scroll of the prophet Isaiah was given to him. He unrolled the scroll and found the place where it was written:

"The Spirit of the Lord is upon me,
    because he has anointed me
        to bring good news to the poor.
He has sent me to proclaim release to the captives
    and recovery of sight to the blind,
        to let the oppressed go free,
to proclaim the year of the Lord's favor."

And he rolled up the scroll, gave it back to the attendant, and sat down. The eyes of all in the synagogue were fixed on him. Then he began to say to them, "Today this scripture has been fulfilled in your hearing." All spoke well of him and were amazed at the gracious words that came from his mouth.

- God defends those whom nobody else defends. Jesus was looking at families that struggled to survive, at people dispossessed of their land, at starving children, at prostitutes and beggars. He never said they were good or virtuous; he said only that they were suffering unjustly. God takes their side! Do I?

- Lord, open my heart to the broken body of Christ revealed in my suffering brothers and sisters. Make me hunger for justice and work for peace. May your compassion be a constant burning fire in my life.

Friday January 8
Luke 5:12–16

Once, when he was in one of the cities, there was a man covered with leprosy. When he saw Jesus, he bowed with his face to the ground and begged him, "Lord, if you choose, you can make me clean." Then Jesus stretched out his hand, touched him, and said, "I do choose. Be made clean." Immediately the leprosy left him. And he ordered him to tell no one. "Go," he said, "and show yourself to the priest, and, as Moses commanded, make an offering for your cleansing, for a testimony to them." But now more than ever the word about Jesus spread abroad; many crowds would gather to hear him and to be cured of their diseases. But he would withdraw to deserted places and pray.

- An energy point for Jesus was his prayer, and we find that at key times of his life, he prayed: before calling the twelve; at the time of temptation and the struggle at his Passion and death; and very often as part of his daily life he went to quiet places to pray. His ministry needed the support and life-giving energy of his relationship with his Father. Our life of love needs the energy of prayer. Prayer enhances family life, friendship, and work or ministry for others. When we bring the love and commitments of our lives to prayer, something happens to bring us deeper into the source of our convictions and commitments to God and others.

Saturday January 9
John 3:22–30

After this Jesus and his disciples went into the Judean countryside, and he spent some time there with them and baptized. John also was baptizing at Aenon near Salim because water was abundant there; and people kept coming and were being baptized—John, of course, had not yet been thrown into prison.

Now a discussion about purification arose between John's disciples and a Jew. They came to John and said to him, "Rabbi, the one who was with you across the Jordan, to whom you testified, here he is baptizing, and all are going to him." John answered, "No one can receive anything except what has been given from heaven. You yourselves are my witnesses that I said, 'I am not the Messiah, but I have been sent ahead of him.' He who has the bride is the bridegroom. The friend of the bridegroom, who stands and hears him, rejoices greatly at the bridegroom's voice. For this reason my joy has been fulfilled. He must increase, but I must decrease."

- This reading marks a stage in the transition from the preaching and ministry of John the Baptist to that of Jesus.

- Some of John's disciples had joined Jesus at John's prompting, "Look, here is the Lamb of God!" (John 1:36). Those that remained with John now seem to be upset that "all" are going to Jesus. John, however, knows that his duty to arrange everything for the wedding of his friend Jesus to his bride, the people of Israel, has been fulfilled. With his mission accomplished, he can retire with joy. He would soon suffer martyrdom (Mark 6:14–29).

- In my life, is Jesus increasing, becoming more and more?

Sunday January 10
The Baptism of the Lord
Mark 1:7–11

He proclaimed, "The one who is more powerful than I is coming after me; I am not worthy to stoop down and untie the thong of his sandals. I have baptised you with water; but he will baptise you with the Holy Spirit."

In those days Jesus came from Nazareth of Galilee and was baptised by John in the Jordan. And just as he was coming up out of the water, he saw the heavens torn apart and the Spirit descending like a dove on him. And a voice came from heaven, "You are my Son, the Beloved; with you I am well pleased."

- Jesus' baptism gives us a window into a powerful religious moment. Jesus knows his identity. The imprint of the Spirit has sealed his life. Lord, remind me that I too bear your seal of approval. I am marked by your Spirit, called to participate in your mission as your beloved son or daughter.

- John knows his identity and his place in the unfolding plan of God. He is the instrument who points people beyond himself toward Jesus. Who are the "John the Baptist" figures in my own life?

An Advent Retreat

A time of retreat offers us many chances: a chance to take a step back from the routine and concerns of our everyday lives; a chance to reflect prayerfully on who and what is really important; a chance to look with honesty at our relationship with people, all of creation, and, especially, to focus on our relationship with God. A retreat give us the chance to ask the question: Do these relationships need more nurturing?

Here is the perfect opportunity to spend some time in the presence of a loving God who is waiting to welcome you, nurture you, and draw you into deeper relationship.

To help and guide us in our prayer and reflection during these weeks, we are looking at the theme of New Beginnings. We look at how our lives can take a completely different path and direction when God enters our story. We remember St. Ignatius of Loyola, who was so convinced of his path in life until the "cannonball moment" in Pamplona. God intervened in his story, and his life took a completely different direction. During this time of Advent, we reflect on the lives of many people in the Scriptures with similar stories. Like Mary, we can have moments of visitation, when our plans are turned upside down for a greater plan. As with Joseph, we can awaken from dreams with a new clarity. And like the Wise Men, we can be drawn to a new place, the dwelling place of God, by the light of a "star." This Advent we invite you to commit some time for stillness and to listen for the voice "crying in the wilderness," some time to become more aware of the opportunities for new beginnings as you walk with God. As we begin our time of retreat, let us focus on God's message to us from the prophet Isaiah: "I am about to do a new thing; now it springs forth, do you not perceive it?" (43:19)

Session 1: New Beginnings with John the Baptist

Invitation to Stillness

Most of us can enter more fully into prayer if we take a little time to become still. At the beginning of each session's prayer, we will suggest a stillness exercise and lead you through it. For today, let's take a few moments to use our breath to enter into stillness. Begin by noticing your breath: the sound of it, and the rhythm. No need to change the rate. Notice the air as it enters your body, fills your lungs, sustains your life, and then departs. As you inhale, breathe in God's love for you. As you exhale, breathe out anything you want to share with God, or anything you want to let go of and hand over to God. Repeat this for three deep breaths. John was a voice in the wilderness. Can you be still enough now to hear his voice in your own wilderness?

Reading

Matthew 3:1–4

In those days John the Baptist appeared in the wilderness of Judea, proclaiming, "Repent, for the kingdom of heaven has come near." This is the one of whom the prophet Isaiah spoke when he said, "The voice of one crying out in the wilderness: 'Prepare the way of the Lord, make his paths straight.'" Now John wore clothing of camel's hair with a leather belt around his waist, and his food was locusts and wild honey.

Reflect

- John the Baptist is an unusual character, and we might find him somewhat off-putting at first glance. Someone who dresses as he does and who eats locusts and wild honey is probably not the kind of person you could imagine wanting to spend time with! But this is true of all great prophetic figures: they make us uncomfortable, they shake us out of our habitual way of seeing things, and they force us to confront those parts of ourselves that we would prefer to ignore. And this is exactly what John's message is: "Repent!" "Turn around!" "Begin again!"

- Writer and teacher Richard Rohr, OFM explains that the word that is usually translated into English as "repent" is a Greek word that really means "turn your mind around" or "change." John wants us to change our way of looking at things, and see ourselves and the world in a different way. He wants us to see ourselves and the world in truth, as they really are, and not the way we imagine them or would like them to be. And he wants this for a very good reason: "the kingdom of heaven has come near." God is about to come and live among us in the human form of Jesus, as one of us.

- God is showing us that our human bodies and souls, imperfect though they may be, are loved by God to the point where God is happy to share them. God wants us to see things as God sees them. Later on, Jesus will try to shake up people's vision of reality. He will tell us (among other things) that God is like the father of the Prodigal Son, never uttering a word of blame, wanting only to celebrate a child's return, loving that child in all his messiness and failure, full of joy that the child has come home again.

Talk to God

- What does a new beginning mean to me today, at this moment, as I am making time to pray? I take a moment to reflect honestly on myself. Are there things about myself that I am afraid to face? What are they? Is there a pattern of unhealthy behavior, an addiction, a toxic relationship? I turn to God, who knows me better than I know myself, and who loves me deeply. I imagine Jesus standing here looking at me with love. I allow that love to touch me. I ask Jesus to help me face those things in myself that need to be brought into the light.

- I take a moment now to look at the people who are close to me—my family, my friends. Is a new beginning possible in any of my relationships? Is there something that needs changing, that needs me to turn my mind around, to change how I see things in that relationship? I bring those I love, those with whom my life is intertwined, into this sacred space before God, and I talk to Jesus about my relationships, about the things I can change and the things I can't change. Sometimes a new beginning in a relationship means accepting that I cannot change another person.

- And now I turn to all those many people who touch my life every day but who are not part of my close circle of friends. I think of work colleagues, people who serve my needs in shops and cafés, homeless people I pass every day on the street, refugees, travelers. What is my attitude to all these people who, like me, are loved by God? Do I treat them with respect and courtesy? Do I judge them? Do I behave arrogantly toward them? Is there a new beginning possible here? I talk to Jesus about my attitude toward other people.

- Finally, I ask God to help me accept myself. I ask God to help me realize how greatly I am loved. I ask for healing, light, hope, and joy. I ask God to show me one small step I can take today toward a new beginning. And then I just spend some quiet time listening to what God has to say to me.

Session 2: New Beginnings with Mary

Invitation to Stillness

For a few moments of stillness, settle yourself into a comfortable position. Close your eyes and imagine all your worries, distractions, and concerns fading away. Allow yourself to become quiet within. Mary's heart was still and open to hear the message of the angel. Listen attentively to the different sounds you hear around you and to the voice within. Maybe you can hear your own heartbeat. As you relax into listening, try to become aware that God is near, within you, speaking a message to you today and making a home in your heart right now. This is a moment of Visitation for you.

Reading

Luke 1:26–38

In the sixth month the angel Gabriel was sent by God to a town in Galilee called Nazareth, to a virgin engaged to a man whose name was Joseph, of the house of David. The virgin's name was Mary. And he came to her and said, "Greetings, favored one! The Lord is with you." But she was much perplexed by his words and pondered what sort of greeting this might be. The angel said to her, "Do not be afraid, Mary, for you have found favor with God. And now, you will conceive in your womb and bear a son, and you will name him Jesus. He will be great, and will be called the Son of the Most High, and the Lord God will give to him the throne of his ancestor David. He will reign over the house of Jacob forever, and of his kingdom there will be no end." Mary said to the angel, "How can this be, since I am a virgin?" The angel said to her, "The Holy Spirit will come upon you, and the power of the Most High will overshadow you; therefore, the child to be born will be holy; he will be called Son of God. And now, your relative Elizabeth in her old age has also conceived a son; and this is the sixth month for her who was said to be barren. For nothing will be impossible with God." Then Mary said, "Here am I, the servant of the Lord; let it be with me according to your word." Then the angel departed from her.

Reflect

- Think about this story for a little while. What must this have been like for Mary? Here was an ordinary young girl, not yet married, who was being told that she was about to become pregnant in a most extraordinary way. One would expect that she would have protested that she could not go through with such a plan. What would she tell her fiancé? What would she tell her parents, the neighbors, other people? What would everyone think? And so on. But all she did was ask a very simple question: "How can this be, since I am a virgin?" Isn't that extraordinary? All she wanted to know was how such a thing was possible. And once the angel had explained to her that this would happen through the power of the Most High, Mary immediately accepted, without a single complaint about all the trouble that it would undoubtedly cause her: "Here am I, the servant of the Lord; let it be with me according to your word."

- Mary's trust in God was so great that she was prepared to put aside all her dreams and plans about how her life would unfold and step out into a place of huge uncertainty, into a situation over which she would have no control. New beginnings can be frightening to us. We like certainty and we do not like stepping outside our comfort zones. Yet that is often the place where the most wonderful things can happen, as Mary's story shows us.

Talk to God

- Since beginning this retreat, have I become aware of the visit of an angel in my own life? Angels come in all shapes and sizes! Have I become aware of any inner invitation to step outside my comfort zone and into the unknown, perhaps by facing up to something unhealthy in my life or in my relationships? Am I perhaps afraid to take the first necessary step? Do I prefer to stay in the safety of what is familiar, even when I can see that things need to change? I talk to God honestly about this, not concealing my fears from God or from myself. I ask for the gift of trust.

- As I reflect on the situation in which Mary found herself, I can see that sometimes a new beginning is hidden in the ending of something else. All the plans Mary must have had for her life had suddenly ended with the angel's visit. I reflect now on times when my life has taken unexpected and unwelcome or alarming turns. Perhaps I have suffered a sudden bereavement, an illness, the breakup of a relationship, the loss of a job, or even the loss of my home. I ask God to help me see the possibility of a new beginning that is hidden in what might seem to be an ending. I ask God to help me accept the twists and turns my life takes.

- An encounter with an angel brings a transformative energy that empowers us. We are not alone. God never asks us to do something on our own but "overshadows" us. Let's sit for a while in silence with God and allow ourselves be overshadowed.

Session 3: New Beginnings with Joseph

Invitation to Stillness

As always, it helps to close your eyes and spend a few moments letting your inner self find some quiet. Take a moment to breathe in the presence of God and breathe out all that troubles you today. Repeat this a few times. You are here to receive some new light on your life and to get in touch with your deeper desires and your dreams. God spoke to Joseph in a dream as he slept and continues to speak to us in many ways. Listen for God's voice in the stillness of your heart now.

Reading

Matthew 1:18–24

Now the birth of Jesus the Messiah took place in this way. When his mother Mary had been engaged to Joseph, but before they lived together, she was found to be with child from the Holy Spirit. Her husband Joseph, being a righteous man and unwilling to expose her to public disgrace, planned to dismiss her quietly. But just when he had resolved to do this, an angel of the Lord appeared to him in a dream and said, "Joseph, son of David, do not be afraid to take Mary as your wife, for the child conceived in her is from the Holy Spirit. She will bear a son, and you are to name him Jesus, for he will save his people from their sins." All this took place to fulfill what had been spoken by the Lord through the prophet: 'Look, the virgin shall conceive and bear a son, and they shall name him Emmanuel,' which means, 'God is with us.'" When Joseph awoke from sleep, he did as the angel of the Lord commanded him; he took her as his wife.

Reflect

- This short Gospel passage reveals a very painful period in the relationship between Mary and Joseph. We don't know whether Mary had tried to explain to Joseph what had happened, or whether she had decided not even to attempt it. What is clear is that Joseph believed Mary had been unfaithful, and he had made up his mind not to marry her. What pain that must have caused each of them: Mary, to feel that the man she loved no longer trusted her; Joseph, to think that the woman he loved was unfaithful. The Gospel doesn't tell us how long this misunderstanding lasted before Joseph was visited by an angel with the truth, but whether the period was long or short, it must have been unbearable for the young couple who had to live through it.

- Most of us have experienced the pain of being misunderstood. Most, if not all of us, have experienced the breakdown of a relationship, whether within our immediate family or with a friend. Perhaps I am even experiencing this right now. I might well ask, Where is the new beginning in such a situation? Where is God in this? Perhaps I can find consolation and encouragement in the fact that even Mary and Joseph, those two most holy people, did not escape this experience. Perhaps I can learn something from how they behaved during it.

Talk to God

- Under the loving gaze of God, I look honestly at my closest familial relationship, whether it is with a spouse, partner, parent, child, or sibling. Is the relationship healthy and loving? If so, I thank God for it. I bring that person into my prayer and hold him or her before the loving gaze of God. I ask God to continue to strengthen us in our mutual love and to preserve us from misjudging or misunderstanding one another.

- If, on the other hand, something has gone wrong in what was once a loving relationship, I now look honestly at the situation. I ask God for light to see the truth. If I have misjudged the other person in any way, I ask God to show that to me and to give me the courage to face it. If I am in any way at fault, is there some step I can take so that we can have a new beginning?

- If, having reflected as honestly as I can on the relationship, I believe that the breakdown has been caused by some betrayal on the part of the other person, and if I feel that the relationship is no longer life-giving for me, how should I approach the situation? I reflect on how Joseph behaved when he felt it necessary to end his relationship with Mary. He did not wish to punish her or to take revenge on her by making the matter public. Again I ask God for light, and for the ability to forgive. I ask for God's grace that any action I feel I may need to take will not be vengeful.

- I sit for some time in silence, allowing God to touch my heart.

Session 4: New Beginnings with Jesus
Invitation to Stillness

Using a mantra can help us find stillness in the busyness of life. Take a few moments to settle yourself into this time of prayer. Notice where you are, how you are, what is going on for you. Give it all to God, then ask for what you seek in this prayer. It might be to know Jesus more as Lord or Messiah or friend, or just more intimately. Take the Aramaic word *Maranatha*, which means "come, O Lord," and repeat it as you breathe. *Maranatha*. Repeat the word for a couple of minutes and, if you become distracted, simply return to the word.

Reading
Luke 2:1–7

In those days a decree went out from Emperor Augustus that all the world should be registered. This was the first registration and was taken while Quirinius was governor of Syria. All went to their own towns to be registered. Joseph also went from the town of Nazareth in Galilee to Judea, to the city of David called Bethlehem, because he was descended from the house and family of David. He went to be registered with Mary, to whom he was engaged and who was expecting a child. While they were there, the time came for her to deliver her child. And she gave birth to her firstborn son and wrapped him in bands of cloth, and laid him in a manger, because there was no place for them in the inn.

Reflect

- And so on this fourth week of Advent, we arrive at the greatest new beginning of all: the birth of Jesus. It was, of course, a new beginning for the whole of humanity because God had come to live among us, as one of us. But, strange as it may sound, it was a new beginning for God too. God is eternal. God never had a beginning and will never have an end. But in the birth of Jesus, God was beginning something new: God was starting to live a human life, with all that it entailed—even death.

- And what does this mean for me? What relevance does this event of over two thousand years ago have for my life now? St. Paul tells us that when God became human in the person of Jesus, Jesus emptied himself of his divinity so that he could fully experience his new humanity. He did not cling to his divinity but became exactly like us. St. Luke tells us that he grew—not only physically, but also in wisdom and knowledge. As God, he knew all things; as a human, he had to learn them, bit by bit, just as we do.

- This total letting-go on the part of Jesus has something to teach me. Do I have a tendency to cling to what is past? Does this prevent me from fully embracing the present moment and all the newness it has to offer? Am I perhaps missing the gifts that God is offering me now, in the present moment, which is the only reality? The past is gone; the future doesn't yet exist. Only in the present will I find God.

Talk to God

- I imagine Jesus sitting here with me. In his presence, I reflect honestly on what might be preventing me from truly beginning again, right now, in this present moment. I ask him to show me whether I am holding on to something that is unhelpful, that is not life-giving, that is perhaps even toxic.

- Am I afraid to let go of some addiction, because life will seem unbearable without it? I ask Jesus to help me trust him enough to take the first small step, whatever it is. It might simply be acknowledging to myself and to someone else that I have an addiction and need help. I ask for the gift of hope, which will allow me to see that a new beginning and a new life are possible.

- Am I holding on to some grudge that is preventing me from fully embracing a new beginning in a relationship that has been damaged? I ask Jesus to help me let go of that comfortable grudge behind which I may be hiding, and for the clarity of vision to see how unhelpful it is.

- Perhaps my life has changed in some way that I find difficult to accept, and I am clinging desperately to a memory of the way things used to be. I talk to Jesus about this, asking for the strength to let go of the past and move into the present, with all its possibilities of new life and greater freedom, if only I can embrace it.

- And now I sit quietly with Jesus and allow him to speak to me and to reassure me that all his gifts are life-giving.

Session 5: New Beginnings with the Wise Men

Invitation to Stillness

As we prepare for our final session, we will focus on stilling the mind. Become aware of the noises around you. Perhaps you can hear traffic in the background or the sounds of nature, maybe the hum of technology in your house or surroundings. Whatever you hear, notice these noises and then let them go. Begin to focus on the simple life-giving breath given to you by God. Take some deep breaths, breathing in all that is life-giving and breathing out all that disturbs. The Wise Men were drawn to God by the light of a star. Can you see it? Sit quietly under the light of this star for a few moments. Allow the star to shine on you, illuminating your path and your innermost being. Gratefully receive all it has to offer you now.

Reading
Matthew 2:1–12

In the time of King Herod, after Jesus was born in Bethlehem of Judea, wise men from the East came to Jerusalem, asking, "Where is the child who has been born king of the Jews? For we observed his star at its rising, and have come to pay him homage." When King Herod heard this, he was frightened, and all Jerusalem with him; and calling together all the chief priests and scribes of the people, he inquired of them where the Messiah was to be born. They told him, "In Bethlehem of Judea; for so it has been written by the prophet:

'And you, Bethlehem, in the land of Judah, are by no means least among the rulers of Judah; for from you shall come a ruler who is to shepherd my people Israel.'"

Then Herod secretly called for the wise men and learned from them the exact time when the star had appeared. Then he sent them to Bethlehem, saying, "Go and search diligently for the child; and when you have found him, bring me word so that I may also go and pay him homage." When they had heard the king, they set out; and there, ahead of them, went the star that they had seen at its rising, until it stopped over the place where the child was. When they saw that the star had stopped, they were overwhelmed with joy. On entering the house, they saw the child with Mary his mother; and they knelt down and paid him homage. Then, opening their treasure chests, they offered him gifts of gold, frankincense, and myrrh. And having been warned in a dream not to return to Herod, they left for their own country by another road.

Reflect

We don't know who these Wise Men were. Tradition refers to them as kings, but the Gospel merely calls them wise men. Whoever they were, they saw a star, and left family and home and all their ordinary preoccupations behind them, and followed it. They believed that the star signified the birth of a great king, and they wished to pay homage to him. They must have been astonished when the star finally stopped and stood over a humble dwelling. They must surely have expected a palace. But they never for a moment doubted that they had come to the right place. They were filled with joy, the Gospel tells us, and they knelt down and paid homage to the baby. They trusted their star, even when it surprised them with the unexpected.

- As I reach the final days of my retreat, can I see the path of a new beginning open out in front of me? Can I see the star that shines over it? What is the star in my life? What is it that excites me and gives me energy and joy? Can I trust it enough to follow it, or am I held back by fear? Can I trust it even when it leads me to a place I was not expecting?

- Can I embark on a new beginning?

Talk to God

- In God's presence, I reflect once again on my life and consider whether there is a star beckoning me somewhere. It might take the form of some person who inspires me, or some life-changing event that indicates another possible path for me, or some encounter. Or it may be none of these, but just some gentle inner urge that will not go away. I can be sure of one thing. If I follow it, it will lead me to God in the end. I ask God to help me recognize the stars in my life (sometimes there is more than one!).

- I recognize the star by the joy that it causes. However, that joy is sometimes almost smothered by fear of the unknown. I ask God to show me where my true joy lies, to show me where I can find what is most life-giving for me, and then to help me trust it and set out on the adventure in spite of my fears. I recall that the Lord is my shepherd, and that I am never alone on the journey.

- I ask God to show me those things in my life that hold me back from following my star—things like my desire for security, for control, for the esteem of others. I ask God to help me let go of anything that holds me back, so that, free and joyful, I can set out on the path of my new beginning.

- And, finally, I sit quietly and allow God to speak to me.

Conclusion

As we come to the conclusion of our Advent Retreat, it is helpful to take some time to look back and notice what stays with you from this special time of prayer. How was your heart moved during this time? Is there a Scripture passage or word that has remained with you? What graces have you received? Can you notice some change in yourself? What was difficult or challenging over the time of retreat? Perhaps it would be helpful to write down any insights you have received, or plans and ideas around new beginnings that may have come to light for you. Can you recall the moments of visitation over these weeks, by which angels have crossed your path? Did you have a cannonball moment? Have you noticed some stars and where they may be leading you?

Jesus desires nothing more than to come into every moment of our lives. Ask him now to help you see all that you have been blessed with and to hold on to these graces. Take some time to thank God for this sacred time you have spent together and how your relationship has deepened. Can you perhaps commit to take some new steps each day to continue to nurture this deepened relationship with God? For God is truly with us—Emmanuel—let us rejoice and be glad!